DEAN'S Gold Star

book of

ANIMALS

Illustrated by J. B. LONG
Verses by HELEN CARROLL

PRINTED IN **DEAN &** **SON Ltd.** GREAT BRITAIN
41/43 Ludgate Hill LONDON EC4

© 1975 DEAN & SON, LTD

603 05777 2

Here's a Leopard, see,
Standing in a tree.
Goodness, what a lot
Of funny spots he's got.

A Panda, black and white,
What a pretty sight,
He's come out to-day,
Lots of games to play.

Here's an Okapi,
He likes to eat
Leaves from the trees—
Isn't he sweet?

These are called Bison.
Once at a zoo,
I saw a Bison—
You may see one, too.

The Beavers *are* busy
Building to-day,
When they have finished,
They'll start to play.

Look at the monkey,
A Mandrill's his name,
He looks as if
He'd like a game.

Here is a Wild Cat.
On a fine night
He loves to roam
Neath the moon's light.

Two Polar Bears—
One's had a swim,
The other is diving,
Just look at him.

Here is a Reindeer
Waiting for you
To look at his picture—
And your friends, too.

What a fine Tiger,
Like a big cat.
Have *you* got a pussy
That sits on a mat?

These two are Otters,
They're having their tea.
They both love fish
As you can see.

J. B. LONG.

This is a Porcupine,
He does look funny,
He lives in a burrow
Just like a bunny.

An Elephant and two Giraffes,
And two Impalas, see,
Going to the water
Cool as cool can be.

The animals are thirsty,
It's very hot. I think
That they will feel better
When they've had a drink.

Two Kangaroos
Off for their tea.
If we ran like that
What fun it would be.

A Wild Boar and babies
Looking for food.
I hope they find it,
And that it tastes good.

Look at the Weasels
Sniffing the air.
I think they're wondering
If someone is there.

Hippo is yawning,
He sleeps in the mud.
How would *you* like to?
I don't think I would.

Here is an Antelope,
What a fine sight.
Look at his coat
As dark as the night.

Look at the Cheetah
As fierce as can be.
I'm sure it doesn't
Make friends easily.

Two jolly Zebras,
One's eating grass.
They'd bound away
If you should pass.

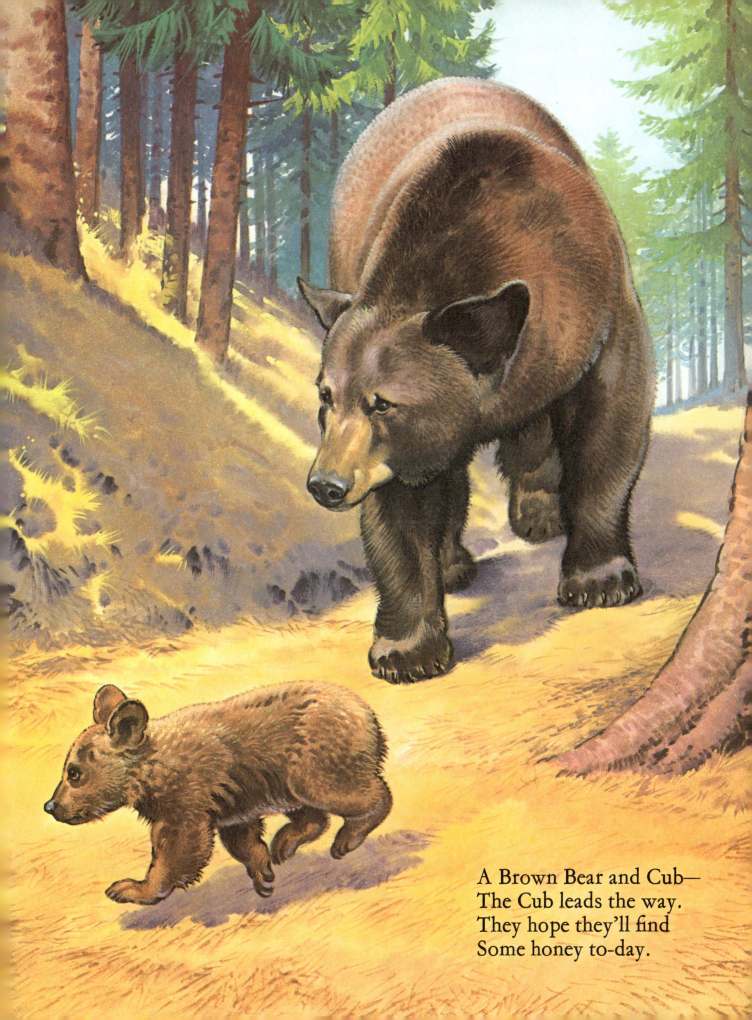

A Brown Bear and Cub—
The Cub leads the way.
They hope they'll find
Some honey to-day.

Rhino's feeling thirsty,
See, the sun shines bright,
A lovely drink of water
Will give him great delight.

Here's a Lion resting,
He is called the King
Of all the Beasts; no wonder
He's proud as anything.

A big Gorilla
On a tree,
He can climb
Quite easily.

Red Deer are beautiful.
They love to roam
Over the hills, but
The forest's their home.

A Puma's a mountain lion,
It *can* become a pet,
They often live in zoos,
Have *you* seen one yet?